Dear Parents and Educators,

Welcome to Penguin Young Readers! As parents and educators, you know that each child develops at their own pace—in terms of speech, critical thinking, and, of course, reading. Penguin Young Readers recognizes this fact. As a result, each Penguin Young Readers book is assigned a traditional easy-to-read level (1–4) as well as an F&P Text Level (A–R). Both of these systems will help you choose the right book for your child. Please refer to the back of each book for specific leveling information. Penguin Young Readers features esteemed authors and illustrators, stories about favorite characters, fascinating nonfiction, and more!

Animal Invaders
Creatures Causing Trouble

LEVEL **4**

F&P TEXT LEVEL **R**

This book is perfect for a **Fluent Reader** who:
- can read the text quickly with minimal effort;
- has good comprehension skills;
- can self-correct (can recognize when something doesn't sound right); and
- can read aloud smoothly and with expression.

Here are some **activities** you can do during and after reading this book:
- Comprehension: After reading the book, answer the following questions:
  - Why were wild boars brought to the United States, and where were they originally from?
  - How many of Guam's bird types have brown tree snakes wiped out?
  - In which oceans do red lionfish live?
- Descriptive Words: A descriptive word is one that points out a specific characteristic of someone or something. The author of this book uses a lot of descriptive words to describe the many sizes these invaders can be and how they look. For example, the cane toad is described as the world's "largest" toad, and Chinese mitten crabs are known for their "fuzzy" front claws. Reread the book, pointing out any descriptive words you see.

Remember, sharing the love of reading with a child is the best gift you can give!

*This book has been officially leveled by using the F&P Text Level Gradient™ leveling system.

For all who move in search of a better life,
may you be welcomed as neighbors—GLC

PENGUIN YOUNG READERS
An imprint of Penguin Random House LLC, New York

First published in the United States of America by Penguin Young Readers,
an imprint of Penguin Random House LLC, New York, 2023

Visit us online at penguinrandomhouse.com.

Library of Congress Control Number: 2023010131

Manufactured in China

ISBN 9780593521946 (pbk)   10 9 8 7 6 5 4 3 2 1 WKT
ISBN 9780593521953 (hc)   10 9 8 7 6 5 4 3 2 1 WKT

PENGUIN YOUNG READERS

LEVEL
FLUENT
READER 4

ANIMAL INVADERS

Creatures Causing Trouble

by Ginjer L. Clarke

Introduction

Every animal has a habitat, or the home where it belongs. But many animals end up living in other places. Sometimes animals have to move to survive. Sometimes people move animals around on purpose or by accident. This can create big problems.

European starlings were brought to New York City in 1890. One man wanted to have birds from England near his home. Now millions of starlings eat seeds and plants on farms all over North America. *Shriek!* They take over nests and steal food from other birds. They spread diseases, too. *Eek!*

These birds and many other creatures are causing trouble. Let's see what these animal invaders are up to.

Mammals Moving In

Wild boars are invaders from Europe, just like starlings. Explorers from Europe brought the boars with them to the United States for food. Now they live in places other than their home habitat and cause harm. These boars are taking over parts of the country, especially in Florida, Texas, and Hawaii.

Dig, dig! Wild boars break up the dirt with their snouts, tusks, and hooves.

They destroy the ground by making
big holes and eating lots of roots. The
boars gobble up almost
anything, including
gardens, grass,
and turtle
nests. What
big pigs!

Nutrias, or river rats, also destroy other animals' habitats. They thrive in rivers and marshes. They have very few predators outside of their native habitat. These giant rodents were taken from South America to the rest of the world. People wanted to sell the nutria's soft fur.

Nutrias have four huge orange front teeth. *Chomp, chomp!* They eat the roots and stems of plants. This kills the plants that provide food, nests, and homes for other animals. Nutrias also chew tires, sprinkler systems, and even wooden siding on houses!

Rhesus macaques (say: REE-suss muh-CACKS) are large, smart monkeys. They are found in many countries in Asia. They live in mountains, forests, grasslands, and cities in large groups called troops.

These monkeys are in Florida, too! A man ran a boat tour on the Silver River in Florida in the 1930s. He put some noisy rhesus monkeys on an island to make the tour fun. *Whoop, whoop!* He thought the monkeys would stay there.

But rhesus monkeys can swim, and a few swam away! Now many troops live in the Silver River area and other parts of Florida. Tourists should not feed, point at, or look directly at the monkeys. They sometimes bite and scratch when they get angry. *Yikes!*

The world's worst animal invaders are rats. *Squeak, squeak!* These pests climb aboard ships and travel everywhere. They especially take over islands where they have no predators but lots of food.

Sugarcane is grown on many islands. Rats love to eat sugarcane. Sugarcane farmers brought another invader to get rid of the rats—Indian gray mongooses. But mongooses are awake during the day, and rats are night creatures. Mongooses hunt small mammals, birds, reptiles, and insects. They eat everything except the rats. *Oh no!*

Another animal that makes trouble is surprising. Cats! All pet cats today are related to wildcats from Africa and Asia. *Meow!* Cats are great pets when kept inside. But house cats that go outside and stray cats with no owners cause big problems.

Stray cats are super invaders in Australia. They even caused some small animals to go extinct. Outdoor house cats in America kill *billions* of birds, mammals, and reptiles each year. A single cat can kill more than 100 animals per year. *Wow!*

Reptiles Roaming

The Everglades is a massive, marshy part of South Florida. It has always been a wild place full of alligators. But now it is even wilder. Huge Burmese pythons from Asia are taking over. *Uh-oh!*

Some pythons were once pets that people dumped in the Everglades when they grew too large to keep. Others came from a big pet store that got destroyed in a hurricane  in 1992. Now these giant snakes are everywhere. *Whoa!*

Scientists believe more than 100,000 pythons now hide, climb, swim, and hunt in the marshes. The pythons eat everything, including large birds, all kinds of mammals, and even alligators!

Far away, another snake is also invading. Guam is an island in the Pacific Ocean. Many planes and ships went there during wartime. Brown tree snakes from Australia accidentally came along for the ride.

Hiss! These venomous snakes are the top predators on the island. They have wiped out 10 of Guam's bird types. *Hush!* Now it is very quiet in the forests there.

The tree snakes move into cities to find food. They slither along power lines and cause power outages. About two million brown tree snakes live on Guam. That is 10 times more than the number of people living there!

Something else is hiding in the trees. Green iguanas! These big lizards from Central and South America can now be found hanging out in Florida and Hawaii.

Look out below! These iguanas sometimes pee or poop on people walking under the trees. *Splat!* The iguanas also sometimes fall out of the trees when it gets very cold.

In the 1980s, many people bought green iguanas as pets. But they let them go when the iguanas got too big. By 2000, South Florida had lots of iguana invaders. *Hello!* They can be spotted basking in the sun on sidewalks, on pool decks, and in driveways.

Black spiny-tailed iguanas are also former pet lizards taking over Florida. They cause big problems on small islands. There are few people but thousands of black iguanas.

These iguanas are the fastest lizards in the world. They can run up to 20 miles per hour! They mainly eat smaller lizards, bird eggs, and sea turtle eggs.

They also like plants in people's gardens and colorful flowers from yards.

Scritch! Scratch! A black iguana digs a burrow. They wreck the concrete under houses and in seawalls. They also damage sand dunes and porch screens. Sometimes they even end up in people's attics! *Surprise!*

Cane toads are the world's largest toads, at more than two pounds. They live in many places all around the world. This is bad news because cane toads are poisonous.

Attack! A snake tries to eat a cane toad. *Get back!* The toad oozes white poison from its skin that kills the snake.

These toads come from Central and South America. They were introduced in the 1930s to Australia, Florida, and some large islands to eat beetles that destroy sugarcane. Now there are billions of toads! The toads did not help solve the beetle problem. And they made a bigger problem by poisoning native predators such as snakes.

Sea Creatures Swarming

Silver carp are raised in fish farms as food in many countries. They are kept in fishponds in the United States to eat the weeds and pests. But many carp escaped in the 1990s when these ponds flooded.

Now lots of silver carp swim in the
Mississippi River and other nearby rivers.
They eat huge amounts of food, so other
fish do not have enough to eat.

Splish, splash! Silver carp leap up to
10 feet out of the water when they are
startled. Sometimes they jump into
fishing boats. *Look out!* These fish are so
big they can even hurt the people in the
boats.

Sea lampreys are also moving in where they do not belong. These long, eel-like fish come from the Atlantic Ocean.

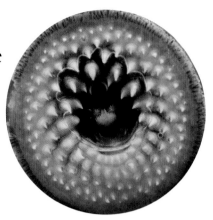

They invaded the Great Lakes through boat canals. Now so many lampreys live in these lakes that they fill up loads of fishing nets. Many other fishes have gone extinct since the lampreys arrived.

A lamprey sneaks up on a bigger fish
in the dark. *Suck!* The lamprey attaches
onto the fish with its round, toothy
mouth. *Slurp!* It drinks the fish's skin and
blood while the fish is still alive! Then
the fish usually dies.

The red lionfish is a fish hunter, too. Its name comes from its fins that look like a lion's mane. It is also called the "firefish." Its poisonous spines sting and burn. *Ow!*

This beautiful but dangerous fish lives in the Pacific and Indian Oceans, but it is popular in aquariums. Many former pet lionfish have been released into the Atlantic Ocean near Florida and the Caribbean. This is bad for swimmers and other fish.

Lionfish attack and eat crabs, shrimp, and fish. A lionfish corners a shrimp with its big, frilly fins. The shrimp cannot escape. *Pow!* The lionfish gulps the shrimp in one bite!

Chinese mitten crabs are named for their fuzzy front claws. These crabs traveled from China to Europe and North America on big ships. They have invaded lots of lakes and rivers, too. How? They can walk on land to go wherever they want. *Skitter, scatter!*

Mitten crabs also burrow in the mud. This harms riverbanks and clogs pipes. They eat many plants and animals, including bait that fishermen use and the fish they catch.

Some people in China eat mitten crabs. But these crabs can carry disease if they are not cooked carefully. *Watch out!*

Zebra mussels also hitched a ride on ships. They moved from the Caspian Sea and the Black Sea in Asia and  Europe to the Great Lakes in North America. They spread quickly and made a big mess.

These shellfish attach to hard surfaces, such as screens, docks, and boat motors. They also block the pipes needed for water systems, hospitals, and power plants.

Pop, pop! Zebra mussels also stick to other mussels and clams, killing them. And they keep the toxins in water in their bodies. This makes birds sick when they eat the shellfish. Mussels cause a lot of trouble!

Insects Invading

Some tiny insect invaders are fire ants. They live in South America but travel around the world on cargo ships. They first arrived in the United States in the early 1900s.

Why are they called fire ants? Because their bites burn and can even kill. *Zip!* Fire ants move in a huge group called a colony. *Zap!* They sting a spider and rip it to pieces.

These fierce fighters eat everything
in their path, including insects, lizards,
and birds. They build a hard mound to
live in, and they especially like fields. Ant
mounds cause a lot of damage to farm
machines.

Fire ants love to
eat ladybugs, or
lady beetles. This
can be a problem.
Lady beetles are
helpful insects that

eat aphids, tiny bugs that harm plants.
Asian lady beetles look the same as
North American ones and were brought
to help control pests. But they eat other
ladybugs, too!

Asian lady beetles also love to eat grapes. This is bad for people who make wine. The beetles crawl inside the grapes and give the wine a bad taste. *Blech!*

These insects also move into people's houses in large groups in cold weather. They smell stinky when they get squished. *Yuck!* And they sometimes bite!

Spongy moth caterpillars were brought to the United States from Europe in 1869. People wanted to sell the silk these caterpillars make. But some caterpillars escaped! Years later, they spread all over the country by hitching rides on cars.

These caterpillars eat tree leaves, which can kill the trees. This also takes away a home for insects, birds, and squirrels. The caterpillars are annoying to people, too. They are covered in stinging hairs that cause rashes when people touch them. *Ouch!*

Emerald ash borer beetles from Asia came to North America in shipping boxes. They were first found in 2002, and they have invaded very quickly. They have already killed millions of ash trees!

Zig, zag! These shiny beetles lay their eggs under the outer bark of ash trees.

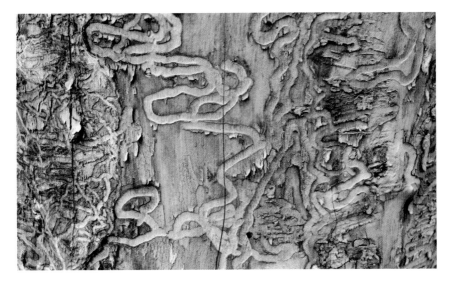

Then the baby beetles hatch and bore, or cut, deep into the inner bark. They eat the trees from inside! The trees die within a couple of years.

We need these trees for wood and paper and to keep forests healthy. Scientists are testing whether some Asian wasps can help control the ash beetles.

Giant African snails are not insects, but they *are* pests. Giant snails are huge! They grow up to eight inches long— about the size of a piece of paper. They invade fast. One snail can lay up to 1,200 eggs per year.

These snails spread across America with some help. A young boy brought three giant snails from a trip in Hawaii back to Florida. He gave them to his grandma to put in her backyard. The snails were all over town in just a few years.

Crunch! These hungry snails eat plants, vegetables, flowers, and tree bark. *Munch!* They even nibble the paint off houses!

Scientists are working on stopping animal invaders from spreading. Humans are the biggest cause of these movements. We can help stop the spreading, too. How?

HELP STOP AQUATIC HITCHHIKERS!

To avoid spreading aquatic invasive species
BEFORE launching ... BEFORE leaving:
- **Remove** aquatic plants and aquatic animals
- **Drain** lake or river water away from the landing
- **Dispose** of unwanted live bait in the trash

It's the Law ... Do Not:
- Transport aquatic plants, zebra mussels, or other prohibited species on public roads
- Launch a watercraft or place a trailer in the water if it has aquatic plants, zebra mussels, or other prohibited species attached
- Transport watercraft without draining water, removing the drain plug, and opening water-draining devices

Minnesota Department of Natural Resources

- Learn about animal and plant invaders in your area, so you can report them.
- Never release any pets into the wild, including fish, birds, and reptiles.
- Keep your pet cat inside your home, and do not feed stray cats.
- Become a volunteer scientist and gather information for studies.

Sometimes animals make trouble. But not all animals that invade new places cause problems. Some are even helpful. Many of them are here to stay. We all need to live together as best we can!